MODERN ARCHITECTURE IN ENGLAND

THE MUSEUM OF MODERN ART · NEW YORK · 1937

REPRINT EDITION, 1969
PUBLISHED FOR THE MUSEUM OF MODERN ART BY ARNO PRESS

Table of Contents

FRONTISPIECE. The Crystal Palace, Hyde Park, 1851, Sydenham, 1854, destroyed by fire, 1936. Designed by Mr. (later Sir) Joseph Paxton; built by Fox, Henderson & Co., under the superintendence of William Cubitt, assisted by Charles H. Wild; decorated by E. Owen Jones.

Acknowledgments

On behalf of the President and Trustees of the Museum of Modern Art, the Director of the Exhibition wishes to thank the architects whose work is included in this exhibition for their cooperation and interest. Acknowledgment is also made to the following for their assistance in assembling information and material:

Hazen Sise; J. M. Richards, Assistant Editor of the Architectural Review, London; G. E. Marfell, Secretary of the Exhibition Committee of the Royal Institute of British Architects; Messrs. P. E. Gane, Ltd., Bristol; Walter Sanders, Associate Editor of the American Architect; Carl Maas, Managing Editor of the American Architect; and Dr. Talbot Hamlin, Librarian of the Avery Architectural Library, Columbia University.

Especial thanks are due:

Professor Henry-Russell Hitchcock, Jr. for contributing the essays on "The British Nineteenth Century and Modern Architecture" and "Modern Architecture in England."

Miss Catherine K. Bauer for contributing the essay on English housing.

Philip R. Rathbone, Assistant General Secretary of the Housing Centre, London, for assembling the material for the housing section of the exhibition.

In connection with this exhibition, a special film of the Zoo buildings by Tecton was prepared by L. Moholy-Nagy. We wish to make grateful acknowledgment to Mr. Moholy-Nagy for the generous contribution of his time and ability to this project; to Cyril Jenkins and Hazen Sise, who acted as his assistants; to The Department of Architecture, Harvard University; the Zoological Society of London; and Tecton for their financial aid; and finally to Professor Joseph Hudnut of Harvard University, Professor Julian Huxley of the Zoological Society of London, L. W. A. T. Drake of Tecton, and Dr. Vevers, Superintendent of the Zoological Society of London for their efforts in helping to make this project a success.

Ernestine M. Fantl, *Director of the Exhibition*

The British Nineteenth Century and

Modern Architecture

I<small>F</small>, in the year 1937, the centenary of Victoria's accession, an exhibition
of Modern British Architecture comes as something of a surprise to many
in America, it is because the generally conservative character of the arts
in Great Britain during the last generation is so well known as to be
exaggerated. The artistic conservatism of the early twentieth century in
Great Britain was in many ways parallel to that of America; but the un-
adventurous consistency of the British architectural scene, unlike the
American, was broken by no such phenomenon as the skyscraper. The
current development in British architecture, to which this exhibition is
devoted, is, therefore, all the more remarkable.

Nineteenth century revivalism and nineteenth century engineering
The historical theory of a British nineteenth century architecture in
which a Gothic Revival succeeded a Classical Revival, only in its turn to
be superseded, after the Queen Anne transition, by a new academicism,
based on seventeenth and eighteenth century forms, has often been attacked in recent years. Yet those who have attacked this theory and have
sought in nineteenth century engineering and esthetic theory for prophecies of modern architecture have sometimes themselves been guilty of

9

distortion by neglecting to analyze the phenomenon of the revivals with an unbiased eye.

Revivalism, obviously, was never what it hoped to be. Revivalists of each generation were the first to cast the stone at the work of their predecessors or to grant them, at best, the merit of having been the first to see the true Greek or the true Gothic or the true Georgian light. But there has been among historians of architecture too little consideration of the possibility that there might be virtues in the very confusion of the revivalists and that there might be found a steady stylistic development behind the kaleidoscopic surface, so patently, if so unsuccessfully, imitated from the past. Perhaps the time is not yet ripe for the presentation of such an hypothesis; nevertheless, the popular tendency to fasten upon the term "Victorian" as having a precise meaning, not equally evident to historical specialists, is perhaps a sign that the architectural production of the nineteenth century will not again be formally presented chiefly as the wreckage of warring creeds.

Revivalism presents a most interesting historical and esthetic problem; but it is more essential here to give once more an account of those rather isolated and still popularly neglected developments which were Great Britain's important early contributions toward the type of architecture we call modern in the mid-twentieth century. This type of architecture crystallized internationally only in the decade after the War, and has been introduced into England in the last few years definitely as a new and Continental development. The mass of contemporary architecture in England which is called traditional represents the last decadence of Victorian revivalism. The new Continental modern architecture which is replacing it has, however, extremely important English roots.[1]

The Crystal Palace

The destruction this fall, ironically by fire, of the Crystal Palace at Sydenham has called public attention to the most prophetic monument of the mid-nineteenth century, a monument often hailed with pardonable exaggeration as the first modern building. The Crystal Palace erected at Sydenham in 1854 was a reconstruction, with the original materials, of the Crystal Palace built for the Great Exhibition of 1851 in Hyde Park

[1] These antecedents have just been revaluated by Nicolaus Pevsner in *Pioneers of the Modern Movement from Morris to Gropius,* London, Faber and Faber, 1936.

10

(frontispiece). Several of the published working drawings of the original Hyde Park structure are included in this exhibition.

The Crystal Palace was the first of a series of buildings which before the end of the century led to the amazing French and German department stores all of glass and iron; but it is insufficiently realized that, in England, it represented not the beginning, but the end of a development. Eastlake in his *History of the Gothic Revival*, 1872, after recounting the popular and even professional enthusiasm for the Crystal Palace and the widespread contemporary belief that it made masonry obsolete, remarks:

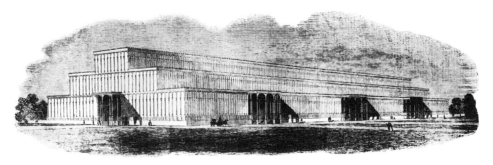

From the Illustrated London News, July 6, 1850

Fig. 2 Paxton, Joseph: Design for the original Crystal Palace for the Great Exhibition of 1851

"It did not take many years to dissipate the dreams of universal philanthropy to which the Exhibition scheme had given rise, and with these dreams the charming visions of a glass-and-iron architecture may also be said to have vanished. If the structural details of the Crystal Palace teach us any lesson, it is that they are strictly limited in application to the purpose for which the building was erected and that even for such a purpose their adoption is not unattended by drawbacks. The Gothic Revival was little affected by the great event of 1851," and Paxton, the architect of the Crystal Palace, was soon "employed on the restoration of a church."!

Railway stations and greenhouses
King's Cross Station, built in 1852, its brick façade as simple and straightforward as the iron and glass roofs of its magnificent train sheds, is almost the only English building of the immediately succeeding period com-

parable with the Crystal Palace in its freedom from revivalism. After King's Cross, the architects had their revivalistic will in the design of most British railroad stations. That some of these buildings with their strange amalgam of ancient forms and modern construction have real architectural virtues one cannot deny; but they are not direct ancestors of modern architecture in the same sense as the Crystal Palace, or even the Gare du Nord in Paris and the Anhalter Bahnhof in Berlin, built in the next two decades.

The line of development toward modern architecture through the bold and imaginative use of metal ended in 1851 in England; but while it lasted it had produced, before the Crystal Palace, a series of monuments of distinction and real beauty. The sequence of great greenhouses, of which the finest is perhaps at Kew, need only be mentioned here, even though the Crystal Palace, as an apotheosis of the greenhouse, far exceeded in every way all preliminary steps; but in the field of bridge design the work of Telford, Brunel and Stephenson must always be rated among the finest monuments in metal, not only of the nineteenth century, but of any age, and it deserves particular discussion.

Bridges

England, as the first country to be extensively industrialized, was naturally the first to avail herself in engineering of the new products of industry. The first cast-iron bridge, at Coalbrookdale in Staffordshire, was built by Wilkinson in the seventies of the eighteenth century. This and the immediately succeeding bridges were of the arched type, and neither conspicuously large nor impressive in design. On the other hand, Thomas Telford's project of 1801 for rebuilding London Bridge with an iron arch of 600 foot span remains one of the most beautiful bridge conceptions ever developed on paper (Fig. 1). The delicate fret work is well suited to the character of metal and exquisitely adjusted to the main curves of the arch. Unfortunately this superb project was never carried out.

Telford's Menai Bridge at Llanfairpwllgwyngyllgogwrychwrndrob-wllllandyslliogogogoch[1] across the Menia Strait between North Wales and the Isle of Anglesey, built 1819-1826, was the first important suspen-

[1] *Sic!*

12

sion bridge in Europe, with a central span of 580 feet. It is still the long-est suspension bridge in Great Britain, 1000 feet in all. It is certainly remarkably beautiful, although, as a result of the classical embellish-ments of an associated architect, it lacks the ultimate simplicity of Robert Stephenson's nearby Britannia Tubular Bridge of 1846-1850, or even of Brunel's more comparable Clifton Suspension Bridge outside Bristol, built 1836-1864. These latter examples of different structural principles indicate the range of structural imagination and the extraordinary archi-tectural sense of the great English engineers of the early nineteenth cen-tury quite as much as Telford's arch project of 1801.

Residential blocks

Beside these monuments designed by engineers the conventional ma-sonry architecture of the first half of the nineteenth century appears timid and without a future. But it would be unjust to pass on without a word about the ingenious residential developments of the time, of which the finest, perhaps, are in the South Kensington and Ladbroke Grove sections of London, in such provincial cities as Edinburgh and Glasgow, and in watering places like Cheltenham and Tunbridge Wells. Without the architectural pomp of the eighteenth century, but with a far freer hand and a juster sense of the need of open spaces among houses, the middle-class terraces and crescents of the late Regency and early Victorian age still provide a sound model for comparable residential developments today. The conception of the small houses as parts of large blocks, simply but handsomely executed in stone or stucco (Fig. 3), the restriction of through traffic routes, the standardization of type combined with the variety of grouping in streets, in squares, in crescents and, best of all, the frequent preservation of park space and the provision of small private gardens opening toward such park space, are a perpetual amazement to modern eyes. More amazing still is the rapidity with which these sound principles were corrupted as they gave way to the later nineteenth cen-tury concept of the garden suburb with its snobbish and spacious pre-tensions of country estate and private mansion reduced to minuscule scale.

The developments before 1850, suburban when they were built, but also urban in the best sense, can only be compared with the most success-

13

ful achievements of modern architecture in the field of middle-class housing. But for each little street of comparably fine modern work there are still acres of sound early nineteenth century work, now largely left to neglect or thoughtless destruction.

Prophecies and the blindness of prophets

The prophecies of modern architecture in the early nineteenth century were for the most part actual achievements, as fine today as when they were built. But in the second half of the century the prophecies were mostly literary, and came to immediate fruition only in the confused architecture of late revivalism. The written prophecies, surprisingly enough, were received very seriously. The ideas of Pugin were developed not only by Ruskin, but perhaps even more intelligently in the writing of G. G. Scott, certainly by any estimate one of the worst practising archi-

Fig. 3 Thomson, Alexander ("Greek"): Moray Place, Strathbungo, Glasgow

tects of the nineteenth century. Even in the case of Morris, who was so great an inspiration to the young men of the nineties on the Continent, the forward-looking ideas, the profound sense of the diseases of nineteenth century architecture and applied art, were never divorced from mediaevalism, never wedded to an appreciation of the achievements of nineteenth century engineering. On the whole it is nearly fair to say that the writings of the theorists did quite as much harm as good in England and that only in other countries could the wheat of their best intentions be separated from the chaff of their perverse prejudice against all aspects of the modern age. Worse than that, although foreigners today respect these men for their real contribution to modern theory, in England they provide rather the ultimate, if almost unconscious, theoretical support of the traditionalists.

Free traditionalism and its decadence

Within England most of the architecture these writers inspired, however free it was from exact imitation of the past (like the best work of Shaw or Webb in the seventies and eighties), must be rated as coming within the broad borders of revivalism, rather than in any way connected with modern architecture as we know it today. It is a curious historical accident that the easy and imaginative traditionalism of these men, so completely preoccupied with the past, when presented on the Continent in the brilliant studies of Muthesius, could act as a solvent of frozen late nineteenth century academicism there. For the merely careless free planning of the English, the picturesque free massing could be interpreted as precedent for a functional asymmetry controlled by a formal esthetic. But as regards England, the Queen Anne group and, most particularly, Norman Shaw are the direct ancestors, not of the modern architecture of the thirties, but of all English traditional architecture of the early twentieth century, from that of Lutyens to that of the speculative builders, which is still the blight of the architectural scene.

In the present introduction it is impossible to do any of these men justice. But despite the irrelevance of their work here, it should be said that it has just as real virtues as that of "Greek" Thomson or Butterfield, who preceded them, or of Voysey or Baillie Scott, who followed after. The latter, unfortunately, are much too near us to be honestly appreciated.

Either one exaggerates the novelty in their work, which is often no more than an extremely simple use of basically traditional means, or else one notices only the extraordinary extent to which their work provides prototypes for the particular tradition, such as it is, in which the present day speculative builder works.

Mackintosh and the Glasgow School of Art

There remains one great man and one great work: C. R. Mackintosh and his Glasgow School of Art. The competition for this was won in 1893; the greater part of the construction dates from 1898-1899; the west wing, including the library, from 1907-1909. This is without doubt a work of importance equal to or greater than the monuments of the early nineteenth century that have been mentioned earlier. Here for the first time an Englishman, or to be more exact, a Scot, consciously created a work of modern architecture, and for his pains remained, but for this building, all but commissionless. Less happy than Frank Lloyd Wright, with whom it is natural to compare him, he was granted not even a decade or two of support and activity. But, like Wright, he was from the first appreciated on the Continent, and with Berlage and Perret, Wagner and Behrens, Van der Velde and Loos, as well as Wright, he must be reckoned as one of the greatest masters of the generation that preceded the establishment of what we know as modern architecture. These men prepared the way for the contemporary style of today, not merely theoretically, or by analogy, but directly, creatively, in the fullest consciousness of what they were doing. Mackintosh was not quite alone in Great Britain, but beside the Glasgow School of Art the best work of C. Harrison Townsend, or Smith and Brewer, seems tentative and timid, associated more with the American and Continental innovations of the eighties than with the new period of creation that began about 1895.

Perhaps the most remarkable thing about Mackintosh's Glasgow School of Art is that, while the west façade now seems to date a little, and, because of its very virtuosity, remains wholly typical of the opening of the twentieth century, the earlier portion of 1898-1899 (Fig. 4), like the Crystal Palace or the great bridges of Telford and Stephenson and Brunel reaches forward to us across the intervening waste of revivalism. Its entrance motif is still related to the tradition-grounded work of Philip

16

Webb, but the structural frankness of the great studio windows and the splendid sense of proportion they display belong to the contemporary cycle of architectural creation. No work of British architecture could more appropriately serve as an introduction to an exhibition of Modern Architecture in England.

HENRY-RUSSELL HITCHCOCK, Jr.

Fig. 4 Mackintosh, C. R.: Glasgow School of Art, 1898-1899

Elements of English Housing Practice

As a vantage point from which to survey the social and economic forces of the past century, their play and interplay, and their net effect on Western civilization, probably few fields are more rewarding than the English housing movement.

It is not merely that every important effort toward reform naturally becomes a battle-ground in the general warfare of those broad group interests which divide society into employer and employed, creditor and debtor, property-owner and tenant, or city and country. "Housing" cuts across more distinct and seemingly separate fields than do most partial reforms. This is one reason for the wide-spread confusion on the subject today in America. Although bad housing conditions are fundamentally a problem of poverty and the distribution of income in a capitalist system, hence a political issue, there are so many additional problems that one's exact stand cannot by any means always be determined by the degree of one's leftness or rightness. There are no quick and easy answers to questions of building technique and site-planning principle, municipal land policy, health restrictions, esthetic form and administrative framework. Specialists in a dozen fields all have their special axes to grind in housing.

Moreover, every lay person has some sort of direct physical experience with houses. This means that everyone, whether he be architect or mortgagee, slum-owner, company-house tenant, doctor, social worker, tax-collector, revolutionist or ordinary voter, has his own opinions, traditional prejudices and ideals on the subject.

Most of these different opinions and viewpoints have a long history behind them. They represent merely the latest expression of movements which have been developing and changing and growing and spreading for generations. Unless one knows something about this history it is almost impossible to understand, for instance, the complex and often seemingly irrelevant declarations made in the name of "housing" at any ordinary Housing Conference, or on such occasions as the hearings on Senator Wagner's Housing Bill last spring. And this history of the mingled forces which make up the housing movement today took place largely in England.

It is generally recognized that the Industrial Revolution, sweeping first across England, had there its most extreme and immoderate results. On the one hand, it washed that little half-island up to the forefront of imperial and international power. But on the other, it created at home such appalling conditions of child labor, of factory servitude, of slum living, of public unhealth, that a generation of energetic and politically powerful reformers and labor organizations have only just begun to break through the pall of Black England.

The classic descriptions of industrial slums are to be found in Friedrich Engels' *The Condition of the Working Classes in England in 1844*. (Today these descriptions fit certain American urban areas more aptly than they do anything remaining in England.) But a great many purple passages on the horrors of the slums can also be found in the utterances of forward-looking Tory orators and preachers of the time. The fact is that a great many things were beginning to make the Conservatives (more cynical and sophisticated than their Liberal brethren, the convinced apostles of *laissez faire*) look at Black England with a new thoughtfulness and fear and a willingness to make a few mild concessions. The Chartist movement, first industrial working-class uprising, had occurred in the 1830's. Then came the Hungry Forties, which culminated in riot and revolution all across the face of Europe. And then, at the end of the forties and in the early fifties, there were the great and devastating cholera epidemics. Once started, the plague hit rich and poor alike, but gradually the doctors and health officers began to make plain that the breeding-place was in the slums. Finally, the general urban health level was such that the physical standards for entry into the army had to be lowered. This was a situation whose seriousness any imperialist could understand.

Thus was ushered in the era of philanthropic "model tenements," of attempts—some abortive and some partially successful—at restrictive legislation, of at least the recognition of "minimum standards." Prince Albert built some model workmen's houses at the Exposition of 1852. The Earl of Shaftesbury devoted half of his life to the passage of the first English Housing Act (the other half he devoted to fighting *against* public education). Disraeli set the pace for Bismarck in paternalistic reform. Many

20

American organizations interested in housing and general social welfare represent this Tory paternalism.

The English Liberals of the Manchester school (and even of the Lloyd George variety) have had mainly a negative influence on the housing movement. They wanted individual home-ownership. And they wanted to keep the government out of it. "Progress," they felt, would solve everything. Leadership in housing reform passed directly from the Conservatives into the hands of the Labor Party, who made it a prime issue in so far as they had power.

The Labor Party organization has always been based primarily on the trade unions. This meant that the Labor Party was able to have a powerful influence in the local politics of industrial cities long before it cut a real figure nationally. In its formative period, its Brain Trusters in matters not directly concerned with wages and working conditions, were the Fabian Socialists. The Fabians were not Marxists; they were embarrassed at the notion of revolutionary fervor or world-shaking presumptions of any kind. But they believed in promoting National Minima—standards of wages, security, sanitation, housing, open space, recreational facilities, education. And they believed in Good Government—in administration by trained professionals, particularly in such urban matters as water supply, sanitation, inspection of houses, public utilities—and also in the extension of public initiative and responsibility, particularly to workers' housing.

In the critical housing shortage just after the war, the Labor Party initiated the first large-scale program of public-aided housing. This program was based on combined State and local subsidies and local initiative. Until quite recently the English housing program has waxed and waned in direct relation to the national and local political fortunes of the Labor Party. By 1932, however, the issue had grown so popular that no party could afford to fight against it. The Conservative National Government has set up somewhat different machinery, and placed much more emphasis on slum clearance, but municipal housing with State aid has continued on quite a large scale. There are now about a million dwellings in England owned and managed by municipal authorities, and within reach—most of them—of working-class families. Moreover, for the first time in any country, a general standard of occupancy which will make room overcrowding illegal and presumably impossible, is gradually being put into effect now.

But England's most characteristic contribution to the modern housing movement must be traced to still another source. The theoretical Utopianism of the 18th century took on much more practical and common-sensible form in England in the 19th. The sketch of a model community which accompanied Robert Owen's famous Plan of 1816 has many features in common with the best "Housing Estates" of today. With its carefully planned factory district and surrounding belt of farms, it is even more directly suggestive of Letchworth and Welwyn, the two Garden Cities. The idea of building an entire new city, with each function analysed in advance and specifically planned for, with the land remaining forever in single ownership, with speculative waste and congestion rendered impossible, and with a broad protecting belt of permanent green open space, has preoccupied many Englishmen—and through ᵗʰem many people all over the world—for several generations. And, although Ebenezer Howard's movement has produced only two actual Garden Cities, it has influenced housing standards and ideals all over the world. It has certainly been largely responsible for the openness and low density of public aided housing in England. ("Garden city lines" means, legally, an average of twelve dwellings per acre.) It has helped to establish the "community" as the unit of new residential construction, with recreational areas and schools planned for from the start. These high space standards are the best things about English housing, and extend to the interior of the dwellings. Five-room houses are pretty much the rule.

In the new physical *technique* of planned large-scale housing development (as distinct from its principles, purposes and politics) , the English contribution has not been so positive. The deep English feeling for land and nature and green open spaces has had its expression not only in space standards and principles of layout but also in town and regional planning progress. But there has been almost no positive expression of new architectural form, however tentative or experimental, within the housing movement. A modern architecture deriving from the new social patterns and planning and housing principles can be found in almost all the Continental countries. The best of these developments actually convince one that an entirely new kind of human environment is not only possible but inevitable. However, if a real modern architecture as an integral part of the housing movement has evolved almost entirely elsewhere, perhaps even here England can claim the timid and tentative first steps. The freshest part of William Morris's theories and the small vital core of the Arts and Crafts Movement found almost no understanding response in England. But in Holland and Germany and Austria the steps from that imported influence up to the clear-cut and often successful architectural experimentation of the past fifteen years are gradual and unbroken.

CATHERINE K. BAUER

Modern Architecture in England

THE International Exhibition of Modern Architecture held at the Museum of Modern Art five years ago consisted in the main of buildings in France, Holland, Germany and America. England was barely represented. Today, it is not altogether an exaggeration to say that England leads the world in modern architectural activity. In part this is because Germany has for political reasons dropped from the running and because in France no conspicuous revival of building has as yet followed on the depression; but even more it is because of the extraordinary rapidity with which an English school of modern architecture has developed in the last two or three years.

It was that unique monument, the Penguin Pond by Lubetkin and Tecton, 1933 (no. *53), which first dramatically attracted the attention of the world to developments in England. With this it became evident that England was not only accepting modern architecture as the logical contemporary way of building, but was providing opportunities for architectural talent of the highest technical and esthetic ingenuity. It could be objected that the Penguin Pond was not in the fullest sense architecture, but rather a large object of abstract sculpture or a permanent stage setting. But anyone who has seen the penguins performing their elaborate music hall turns upon its inclined planes soon realizes that this is no objection: to provide a perfect setting for these incredible creatures, in the London Zoo with its enormous popular audience, was the essential functional problem. Very shortly, moreover, the Highpoint apartment house (no. *54), one of the finest, if not absolutely the finest, middle-class housing projects in the world, gave proof that Lubetkin and his associates were not limited in their mastery to the special field of Zoo design.

An architectural revolution

Once the Penguin Pond had again attracted attention to England (in those years after 1931 when low-cost housing, England's most interesting post-War architectural activity, was in the dumps) it became evident that an able group of young English architects, unconnected with Lubetkin

25

and Tecton, were also well started upon promising careers. Further, several long-established firms were turning more and more successfully to young designers or to new modes of expression of their own in an effort to bring their work into line with the most advanced architecture of the Continent. As economic recovery in the building industry continued it was clear that something of a revolution had taken place in English architecture.

Partly to emphasize the dramatic suddenness of this present development, and partly to do justice to those who, in the late twenties and in the early thirties, took the first steps away from traditionalism and semi-modernism, a brief summary of what has gone on in the last ten or more years is in order before analyzing the existing modern architecture in England to which the exhibition is devoted. If the intrinsic interest of such an account will be for many but slight, it should, none-the-less, serve as an augury that with the revival of building activity in America we may hope for some such architectural revival as England has had.

The late twenties

Modern architecture had won a foothold in England as in America before the depression began, but the newer English architecture of the late twenties reflected chiefly a European half-modernism already past its prime. The principal works of this European half-modernism were constantly appearing in the architectural magazines, while, at the same time, the various Continental schools were being popularized in the books written or sponsored by Yerbury of the Architectural Association.[1]

Yerbury's *Modern European Buildings* of 1928 included, along with foreign examples of recently erected and supposedly modern buildings, Tait's Adelaide House and Emberton's Summit House of 1926. These buildings, marked chiefly by a heaviness derived from contemporary German design, were superior to the American Carrère and Hastings' Devonshire House in Piccadilly. They were, however, only slightly better than Bush House, by Helmle and Corbett, or Ideal House, by Hood and Jeeves, the other outstanding examples of contemporary London

[1] *Swedish Architecture of the Twentieth Century,* and *Modern Architecture in Denmark,* 1925; *Dutch Architecture of the Twentieth Century,* 1926; *Examples of Modern French Architecture,* and *Modern European Buildings,* 1928. It is significant that in the same years Yerbury was also publishing books on Georgian, Spanish and old Dutch architecture.

work by the generally admired American architects. Yet all these works seem far less related to the developed modern architcture now current in England than such an excellent half-modern building as Berlage's Holland House of 1914, to which they bear a certain resemblance.

Even the Royal Horticultural Society building by Easton and Robertson, also published by Yerbury, failed to forecast the future. The exterior is without distinction or interest; the fine interior with its bold concrete arches and mounting clerestoreys is a very close copy of Bjerke's concert hall at the Gothenburg exposition of 1923 in Sweden. Thus, despite the brilliance of the structure, it must be considered as the most successful production of the first wave of post-War European influence rather than as prophetic of what has developed in England since.

This is not the case with New Ways, a house built at Northampton in 1925 by Behrens, the greatest German architect of the older generation. Nor is it true of the Morden Tube Station built by Adams, Holden and Pearson in the following year. Behrens' house, with its horizontally grouped windows, its plain stucco surfaces and rigidly geometrical design, was influenced by the work of such younger men as his distinguished pupil, Gropius. It is certainly one of his most advanced non-industrial works and genuinely prophetic—despite its triangular bay window and the curious ornamental features above the sky line. The Tube Station was, as the product of a native firm, even more significant, although perhaps less conscious of its modernism. It remains on the whole a very successful work of semi-industrial architecture, the first of a series of stations for the London Underground of which several later examples are included in the exhibition (nos. 69-77).

The work of Le Corbusier and the other more progressive Continental architects of the twenties had not been unknown in England, but in 1927 Frederick Etchell's English translation of *Vers Une Architecture,* by Le Corbusier, provided the first impressive literary presentation of the theories and accomplishments of the most advanced European architecture. Bennett's *Architectural Design in Concrete,* published in the same year, indicated a growing awareness among English technicians of the possibilities inherent in the bold use of new materials. *The Architectural Review,* perhaps the leading English periodical, published an extremely favorable review of Etchell's translation as well as editorials about and

27

articles by Le Corbusier. Le Corbusier was referred to as "the best archi-tect alive" by Raymond Mortimer in the *Nation and Athenaeum* review of the architect's *Urbanisme,* which was brought out in translation the next year.

In 1928 a group of houses built by Tait for the Crittall Metal Window Company, although extremely tentative and hybrid in their inspiration, represented perhaps the first reflection of the newer architectural ideals of the Continent in actual building by Englishmen[1] in England. Only one of these houses, most inappropriately known as "Le Château," bears examination today. None-the-less the experiment indicated, even more than did the same architect's Adelaide House, the open-mindedness of Tait, the active member in one of the largest and most successful archi-tectural firms in England. It was evidence also of industry's sponsorship of new architectural ideals—an inclination fostered in part at least by Le Corbusier's ideas on standardization of parts.[2]

The early thirties

The Royal Corinthian Yacht Club at Burnham-on-Crouch, built by Emberton in 1930-31, in the lightness of its construction and in its straightforward design represents an extraordinary advance over his Empire Hall at Olympia, built the previous year.[3] The Yacht Club, despite certain clumsy details, was a really sound piece of modern archi-tecture. As such it represented England in the International Exhibition of Modern Architecture held at the Museum of Modern Art in 1932, together with High-and-over, a large country house at Amersham by Connell and Ward, in which the rather doctrinaire acceptance of mod-ern principles was combined with an arbitrarily brutal sense of form.

The Daily Express Building in Fleet Street, of 1931-32, for whose bold cantilevering the engineer Sir E. Owen Williams was chiefly responsible, was probably the most striking of the other modern buildings erected in England at that time. Although this appeared and still appears like a

[1] Or is it significant that Tait came from Scotland?

[2] See Hitchcock, Henry-Russell, Jr., "L'Architecture Contemporaine en Angleterre," in *Cahiers d'Art,* 1928, pp. 443-446. In retrospect the polite optimism of the conclusion almost appears prophetic!

[3] This had provided a peculiarly disturbing example of the potentially sinister influence of even so sound a Dutch work as Wils' Amsterdam Stadium.

breath of fresh air in the eclectic confusion of Fleet Street, its enormous areas of black glass taped off with white metal suggest a colossal parody of contemporary American shop fronts. Etchell's less conspicuous office building for Crawford's Advertising Agency in High Holborn, of 1930-31, far surpassed the Daily Express building in intelligence and distinction and might well have found a place in this exhibition. It is certainly wearing far better than most London street architecture of the last hundred years.

Since 1931 Etchell's, unfortunately, has almost given up practice. The major works of Sir John Burnet, Tait and Lorne, and Adams, Holden and Pearson did not for some years develop the promise (such as it was) of the Morden Tube Station and Le Château at Silverend. The works of Sir E. Owen Williams have remained ambiguous: brilliant in their engineering, undistinguished and confused in their architectural expression. On the whole, this was also the case with Emberton. A new generation was destined to come to the fore as a group only with the revival of building in the last three or four years. With the exception of Connell and Ward, who were already in active practice, the younger men in the early thirties had just begun to find work in remodelling and on interiors such as those of the British Broadcasting Company.

Dutch and German influence

This prologue to modern architecture in England may be closed with a word about the sources, other than the ideas and work of Le Corbusier, which in England as in America played some part at this embryonic stage. An article on Gropius' work had been published as early as 1924 in the *Architectural Review;* an English edition of Mendelsohn's *Structures and Sketches* had appeared in 1925. But in both cases the moment was too early. The German influence, like that of the more advanced Dutch architects,[1] was less clear-cut and less pure than that which entered England with the writings of Le Corbusier.

No one could confuse the architectural concepts of Le Corbusier with the turgid decorative aftermath of the Paris Exposition of 1925 which was, superficially, still very influential in England at the opening of the

---

[1] Who were receiving increasing attention—in Yerbury's *Modern Dutch Buildings* of 1931, for example.

thirties. Thus Lubetkin, whose esthetic researches and sense of form were obviously related to those of Le Corbusier, encountered less distrust in the architecturally-minded British public than he might have if the German *Sachlichkeit* of the late twenties had been equally well known and generally accepted in doctrinaire form. The more serene and almost classic modernism of the Dutch Oud and the German Miës van der Rohe were also at this time less familiar in England than in America.

Personnel

If the term "International Style" be open to just criticism as a phrase applied to modern architecture in general, it is, nevertheless, peculiarly descriptive of the current English scene. To London, even before the depression showed signs of lifting, Lubetkin came, drawn from Paris where construction had all but ceased. Later Gropius, Mendelsohn, Breuer and Kaufmann, to mention but the best known, came from Germany, after the revolution of 1933 cut off in its prime the largest and most materially successful school of modern architecture in the world. Lescaze, from America, was also active in England from 1931 on.

Yet, for all its international personnel, the English school of architecture must not be considered an alien phenomenon. Lubetkin from the first has worked not alone but as head of the Tecton group, all of whom are English and several of whom have already broken away to work by themselves. The particular virtues of Tecton's work are not due solely to Lubetkin's foreign origin and training. Gropius' partner, Maxwell Fry, is one of the ablest younger Englishmen and Gropius' English work is possibly inferior to what Fry has done alone (Levy house, no. *28; Hampstead house, no. *22). Breuer's associate, F.R.S. Yorke, is well known for his book, *The Modern House,* published in 1934. Chermayeff, until very recently Mendelsohn's partner, is also a foreigner, but he had been educated in England and had established himself as a modern decorator long before Mendelsohn came to England. The joint work of the two men has been in general superior to what Mendelsohn had done alone in Germany. Lescaze has of late had an English collaborator in Henning.

It can thus be seen that it is artificial and misleading to make a sharp distinction between the current work of the foreign-born architects and

30

that of men like Connell, Ward and Lucas, or Wells Coates, who themselves owe their architectural principles ultimately to the Continent. The English school of modern architecture may therefore be fairly considered as a coherent entity. It is true that certain long established firms, perhaps intending merely to take advantage of a current mode, produce buildings which reveal no thorough comprehension of the basic principles of modern architecture, even while they superficially follow advanced contemporary design. Such work naturally does not possess the intrinsic worth which characterizes the truly modern school. Yet its substitution for the previously popular Swedish and Dutch half-modernism is a significant sign. Work of this sort is already improving more rapidly than similar work in America. In time it may well play an important part in the development of a somewhat more localized variant of the "International Style" than exists in Great Britain as yet.

Clientele

Since English modern architecture has developed in a period of economic recovery, the types of building which the architects have been asked to provide have rarely been of advanced sociological interest. Middle-class houses and apartments, large stores, recreational structures, casinos, cinemas, zoos, schools and factories, rather than low-cost housing, have been demanded.

Since the practice of modern architecture is concentrated in London, its patrons have been chiefly metropolitan but not mainly of foreign origin.[1] While it would be absurd to say that the predominant conservatism of English taste had been basically modified, the public support of modern building seems assured. The immense popularity of the London Zoo buildings testifies to a wide appreciation among classes who have at the present no very direct control of architecture; stores such as Simpson's (no. *18) and apartments such as Athenaeum Court, both in Piccadilly, indicate that the upper classes form no frozen opposition. The discrimination of the lower middle classes is difficult to gauge, but the probability is that if the speculative builders would employ good modern architects, their products would sell as well or better than they do now.

---

[1] The Zoological Society of London, Julian Huxley, Augustus John, Benn Levy, Charles Laughton, Lord de la Warr, Lord Dudley, to mention a few of the more prominent.

Connell and Ward's early and extremely doctrinaire small houses at Amersham, now empty, are not a fair case in point.

Building authorities are still unsympathetic and arbitrary to the point of whimsy in their rulings; but in the first experimental stages of modern architecture in England their instinctive opposition may have been partially justifiable. There is no question, however, that those who think of contemporary building primarily in terms of amenity and sentimental consideration for the existing monuments of the past are neither sympathetic to nor understanding of modern architecture. They permit such a monstrosity of traditionalism as Sir Herbert Baker's new Bank of England to destroy all that was finest of Soane's neo-classic masterpiece, and applaud such another prominent eyesore as the same architect's South Africa House in Trafalgar Square. Yet they make little or no distinction between the most outrageous pseudo-Egyptian factories and the many modern houses shown in this exhibition whose architectural quality would be distinguished anywhere in the world. The British public has proved effectively open-minded in patronizing modern architecture. One might now hope that the general esthetic forces of the nation may soon be educated and mustered for a solid front. Then the good work of the past would still receive its due—which it does not always today—and the good work of the present would be supported against blatant revivalism, sickly traditionalism, and pseudo-modernism.

Urbanism

Although the modern architects of England are clearly aware of the need for new concepts of community design, they have thus far been able to do little or nothing about it. In the London district two problems are not in the least solved or even particularly taken into account by the current modern buildings. First, the rise in the city building heights has created increasing congestion which can ultimately be relieved only by the replanning of whole quarters, providing new open space for the great numbers of people that can be housed in taller buildings.[1] In the second place, the spread of detached and semi-detached villa regions is filling up the home counties in their entirety. Such suburban middle-class

[1] This is well suggested in the project of Breuer and Yorke, published in the *Architectural Record,* November, 1936.

apartment developments as Lubetkin and Tecton's at Highpoint (no. *54) and Gibberd's at Streatham (no. *27) represent an important step in the right direction. Gropius' more ambitious project for country apartment houses to be erected in the magnificent private estates that are perpetually coming on the market would preserve their integrity as landscape instead of breaking them up into garden suburbs of small lots.[1] Even for the middle classes the farce of individualistic housing in the suburbs must give way to some sort of collectivism, as it is already doing in the apartments of the West End. Otherwise the entire southeast of England will become one unbroken dormitory of two-storey villas.

The new Zoos at Whipsnade (nos. 55-*59) and Dudley, and summer resorts, such as Morecambe or Frinton, indicate ideals of planning in terms of counties and even of the whole country rather than in terms of existing cities. Decentralization and managed relocation of industry, such as an intelligent program for the depressed areas of the North, of Scotland and of South Wales would certainly entail, might well provide opportunities for contemporary urbanism and architecture on an unimagined scale.

Structure and Technics

Modern architecture in England provides no particularly important local developments in structure, although the Tecton group has made ingenious use of pre-cast concrete elements in combination with other types of construction (Lubetkin house, no. *60, Weekend house, no. *61, North Gate, Regent's Park Zoo, no. *62). As on the Continent, ferro-concrete is used with far greater virtuosity than in America (Penguin Pond, no. *53, North Gate, Regent's Park Zoo, no *62, Augustus John's Studio, no. *44, etc.). But, on the whole, the conflict between the use of concrete or metal construction, with its obvious advantages, and traditional methods, with their sentimental and labor union backing, is much the same as in America. The chief difference is that light wooden construction, the chief traditional method in America, appears in England rather as an innovation (House on Lloyd George estate, no. *9). It is sponsored by some modern architects as an economical solution of certain architectural problems, and is fortunately unhampered by the associa-

[1] Published in the *Architectural Review*, May, 1935.

33

tion with traditional forms which makes it a brake upon modern development in America.

English plumbing, need it be said, is inferior to American both in the standards currently existing and the fixtures obtainable. In the field of lighting fixtures, however, and hardware[1] in general, satisfactory modern types are apparently cheaper and more readily obtainable. Radiant heating from ceiling panels is possibly a desirable alternative to the complicated and expensive methods of air-conditioning which are increasingly in demand in America. But here the well-known difference between the nations in the matter of preferred temperatures must always play an important part. In reaction to the traditional English method of room heating by coal-burning fires (still required in many low-cost housing projects, it is interesting to note) modern architects seem unduly pleased with visible electrical units (Wells Coates' apartment, no. 14; Highpoint interior, no. 54). These may provide the needed extra heat in a room that is in use, but certainly they have little of the psychological value of a coal- or wood-burning fireplace as a social focus.

English metal windows are admirable and generally better than American. The windows at Highpoint (no. 54) are particularly interesting, folding back like a screen to provide a continuous opening the whole length of the room. Other technical matters of interest may be better discussed under materials. The workmanship of modern buildings, particularly those of a few years ago, is extremely poor, but this has now been very largely remedied.

Materials

Surfacing materials are for several reasons the most difficult elements for the modern architect in England. In the London area various types of stucco and cement rendering[2] have proved terrifyingly receptive to the grime of the metropolitan air. Doubtless they might in the course of several decades reach that ultimate blackness which is not altogether unpleasant in the older brick architecture of London. But after a year or two the effect is extremely disagreeable and a very bad advertisement for modern architecture. It is to be hoped that the mica renderings (no. *28,

[1] There is an excellent line, designed by Wells Coates, in mass production.
[2] Rendered surface; an applied finishing surface of concrete, stucco, mica and concrete mixtures, etc.

34

no. *43) and the smooth concrete surfaces obtained with metal forms, now being introduced in Adie, Button and Partners' Athenaeum Court, will in part solve this problem. In the meantime the grey brick of Tait's Lowndes Street Apartments (no. 5) seems likely to weather more gracefully. In the country, rendered surfaces are by no means unsuitable and in many districts more or less traditional. The building authorities, however, appear prejudiced against them. It is not altogether evident, however, that Fry's Chipperfield house (nos. 20, 21), which he was forced by the authorities to surface with brick and wood, is not as satisfactory as it would have been with the concrete or rendering which he had intended to use.

The conspicuous and ubiquitous misdeeds of the speculative builders, the excessively romantic patina to which the English climate soon reduces all natural materials, and the logical desire for clear light colors in association with clear light forms have, possibly, raised a somewhat exaggerated impasse for the moment over the issue of surfacing materials. Unless surfaces are to be painted frequently, like the stucco work of Regency London (which means a considerable cost for maintenance), the building authorities may perhaps be justified in opposing exposed concrete or stucco rendering. Although modern buildings with brick, tile or stone surfaces will at first be less effective as propaganda than those covered with light-colored rendering, they will probably grow old more gracefully. Le Corbusier points out in his new book, *Quand les Cathédrales Etaient Blanches,* that the medieval cathedrals were once white; it is perhaps as well for us to remind ourselves that modern architecture cannot always remain brand new.

For this reason the increasing use of brick by Tecton, the use of wood by Lescaze's partner, Henning, and above all the use of rough stone by Breuer in the Pavilion at the Royal Show in Bristol (no. *2) are significant. The mere association of certain materials with traditional architecture should no longer be a bar to their use in modern architecture when they are technically suitable. Moderate sized semi-glazed tile units which could be washed would be best for London buildings if they could compete economically with brick or rendering or unfaced concrete. As they are in use in provincial cities for much modern commercial building otherwise of no interest, it is difficult to understand why they have

35

not been adopted by any of the architects now working in London.[1]

Color

Associated with this question of materials is the question of color. The English, still in violent reaction against decadent traditionalism and extremely impressed by Continental achievements during the twenties, are timid and unimaginative in their use of color. Cream color, pale blue, earthy red, blond wood, is almost the total gamut they permit themselves in modern work. Their effects in this respect usually appear rather conventional to American eyes even when they are successful. A return to the use of natural materials of varied even if less pure tones, the introduction of more dark, strong, rich colors might be a desirable development, particularly as it is the light colors now favored which stand up least well against grime.

On the other hand, the English have abused white metals less than Americans (the chief decorative external use of chromium in a building of real quality dates back to Etchell's Crawford's Building of 1930-31). Their predilection for blond wood coloring is soundly based upon the Finnish birch veneer furniture designed by Aalto which is readily obtainable in London (Highpoint interior, no. *54) and on the extraordinarily handsome light cork tiling they use so much for floors. Thanks to the stock furniture,[2] and despite the banality of the coloring, modern English interiors maintain a rather high level of excellence, even where the furniture is not specially designed by the architects (Highpoint interior, no. *54).

Planning

On the whole the planning of the architects of strictly English background is inferior to that of the men who have settled in England after Continental experience. A developed sense of form expressed in clear and simple planning is very evident in the work of Lubetkin (Highpoint,

---

[1] The reason is, perhaps, that the tile-surfaced buildings of the twenties, such as Summit House, are not altogether happy examples.

[2] The furniture designed by Breuer in metal and plywood, despite his long preoccupation with furniture, is less satisfactory than the imported Finnish product. Of the other modern furniture, sponsored by Heal in an exhibition last summer, even the very excellent garden articles by Christopher Nicholson in metal and elm are excessively expensive. However, some items in Heal's regular stock, so simplified as to be no longer traditional, are excellent, as are many purveyed by Gordon Russell (whose shop, by Jellicoe, it may be parenthetically remarked, has the best modern front in London).

no. *54) and Harding (Farnham Common, no. *30). But, in general, one sees a carelessness, due in part to an inadequate sense of space composition and in part merely to the lack of sufficiently detailed study. Conciseness and ingenuity are sometimes quite absent and sometimes exaggerated, while a picturesque confusion related to that of existing English traditionalism is often evident (Lowndes Street Apartments, no. 5; Embassy Court, no. *12; Levy House, no. *28). A general criticism of planning is, however, rather meaningless without a detailed consideration of special problems involved in individual cases.[1]

Sense of form

Curiously enough the sense of form as expressed in the exterior composition of English modern architecture is often of a far higher quality than the plans would lead one to expect. What tends to be lacking in contemporary English architecture is the quality of serenity and classic simplicity particularly associated on the Continent with Oud and Miës van der Rohe. The more doctrinaire men, usually functionalists in theory, are often content with compositions of a somewhat crude and brutal order, in which complexity and even confusion arise, as in the planning, from a lack of esthetic principle and an insufficiency of study. But other men, with backgrounds and training as different as Lubetkin and his group on the one hand (Zoo buildings, nos. *52-*59), and Tait and Oliver Hill on the other (Lowndes Street no. 5, Wentworth house, no. *31), aim at and often achieve brilliant effects in which the use of curves plays a very important part.

Some have assumed that the bold use of curved forms was the particular perquisite of Lubetkin and the other men of Tecton, with whom it is carefully studied and usually controlled by an almost classic discipline. But it must conform to some general demand of the current English situation. If less successful it is equally evident in the work of Tait or Hill, and can be seen almost at its best in the ingenious adaptation of the Peter Jones Store (no. *51) to a difficult site on Sloane Square. For this the young designer Crabtree, working with Slater and Moberly, is responsible. In very different ways, moreover, both Gropius, who rarely used curves in his German work, and Mendelsohn, who abused them in

---

[1] Some of the complexities of Gropius' Levy house, for example, were forced on him by the client.

his Expressionist days fifteen years ago, have in their English work (Levy house, no. *28, Bexhill pavilion, no. *41) broken with rectangularity, often to excellent effect.

In part this romantic elaboration of modern architecture away from the predominantly cubic forms of the twenties can be considered international, but it seems today particularly characteristic of England, perhaps because of the really remarkable success Lubetkin has had with it. It may well be that the more expansive and positive frame of creation which the free use of curves (in plan, in elevation and in section) provides will better suit the English temperament than the mere restraint of doctrinaire functionalism uncontrolled by a real sense of purity of form and an instinct for perfection of proportions. Certainly the immense superiority of Wells Coates' own apartment (no. 14) over such earlier work of his as Embassy Court in Brighton (no. *12) is in very large part due to the ingenuity and elegance in the use of curved and oblique forms as well as to the superior execution.

There can be no question that in England as elsewhere in the world a large part of the earlier modern architecture is, as regards its esthetic character, of chiefly negative significance, a purging of traditional forms from the architectural vocabulary. Once the effectiveness of such a protest is weakened by repetition, a more positive sense of style becomes essential. This Lubetkin certainly has already achieved. The sense of style may well become more general and more versatile in England as the esthetic ideas of others crystallize, partly in sympathy, partly in opposition to what is already recognizable as the Tecton manner. For if the details are always interesting in the work of Tecton, or in such an interior as Wells Coates' apartment, it is because they flow logically from some central principle of design. If on the other hand they are sometimes disappointing, as in much of the work of Connell, Ward and Lucas, and some of Lescaze's, or in that of most of the men converted from traditional architecture, it is because the central principles of design are not altogether clear or sufficiently coherent.[1]

It has been impossible in this discussion to include specific references

[1] It is sad that today both Tait and Emberton, who were the first in England to attempt with any consistency the use of the forms of modern architecture, must be rated as "converts," so much higher is the standard now maintained by the younger men.

to all the buildings illustrated in the catalog. Moreover, some of the references to virtues or faults of individual works illustrated may appear dogmatic or invidious. They are intended merely to suggest the visual meaning behind the critical phrases used. The general excellence of the great majority of the work included is naturally taken for granted.

Comparison with America

For quantity of sound modern building and for quality as well, the English school is certainly ahead of the American. Moreover, we must share with England credit for the work of Lescaze, the man who is easily the most prominent modern architect in the East. Also we have no single architect of the present active generation as distinguished as Lubetkin, nor have we as yet the honor of harboring foreign refugees as important historically as Gropius and Mendelsohn, or as promising as Breuer. One can make these comparisons, however, without rancor, since it is justifiable to hope that through our own building recovery, which is following some two years after that of England, we may hope for a comparable development of modern architecture in the immediate future. Lescaze's more important work is certainly here in America; Neutra has established himself in California and is now being called on for work in the East; many young men are active on excellent housing projects; Rockefeller Center in its extension begins to represent more and more clearly a reflection of possibilities of urbanism long imagined in Europe. Finally, it is the privilege of this catalog to announce that Gropius has accepted the position of Nelson Robinson, Jr. Professor of Architecture at Harvard.

Obstacles and difficulties

But the work of the English contemporary school in the last few years, still so evidently expanding and improving, sets a mark which we will not easily pass in America. It sets that mark, moreover, under cultural conditions more like our own than those of most other countries of the world. We can understand what the obstacles have been in the way of these men, what temptations to compromise, what general distrust, what whimsical building regulations, what indifference to earlier national steps toward modern architecture[1] they have had to overcome. The psychol-

---

[1] Such as those mentioned in the historical introduction to this catalog.

ogy of recovery is generally conservative rather than experimental, and in a world of rising nationalistic prejudice England's hospitality not only to Continental ideas but to foreign architects has been both amazing and profoundly heartening.

Evaluation

An arbitrary and even a dogmatic standard of evaluation—at best no more than a yardstick—is provided by a comparison of the English material illustrated in this catalog with that selected from the work of the entire world and illustrated in the catalog of the International Exhibition of Modern Architecture five years ago. From this it is evident that the bulk of the material in the present exhibition, had it been in existence, would have properly belonged with the work then shown. The evidences of basic creative innovation are of course very much less: the twenties were the period when a new architecture was coming into existence; the thirties are the period of its extension and development. But both the coherence and the variety of the current English work are indicative of a real vitality. The most rigid list of the fine modern buildings of the last few years throughout the world would certainly include several of the Zoo buildings of Lubetkin and Tecton, their Highpoint apartment house, Mendelsohn and Chermayeff's Bexhill pavilion, and the Peter Jones Store of Crabtree, associated with Slater and Moberly. It is right that the work of men of foreign experience should predominate, when one considers that the existence of modern architecture on the Continent goes back some fifteen years and in England hardly more than five. But one feels assured that other men now working in England, whose present buildings are perhaps still tentative in some respects, will forge to the front in the immediate future. It is certain, too, that without losing its coherence with the modern architecture of the rest of the world, the work of the English school will grow more integrated with itself, the difference less marked between the buildings of established firms like Sir John Burnet, Tait and Lorne, or Adams, Holden and Pearson, great engineers like Sir E. Owen Williams, the younger men like Breuer and Yorke, Harding and Samuel, Chitty, Pilichowski and the many men outside London who are just beginning to make themselves known.

40

English Characteristics and Potentialities

Although it sounds like a paradox, it can also be said that the successful establishment of modern architecture in England as an "International Style" should augur the rapid creation there of a firmly national style such as evolved in the seventeenth century. At that time the international academic manner, taken over from Palladio by Inigo Jones and introduced into England by him, led in the mid-century to a new and vigorous national school, including Jones' son-in-law, Webb, Roger Pratt and Hugh May. Some indications of the direction this national trend may well take are suggested in early portions of this text: the development of the free use of curves; the return in part to the use of natural materials, the extension of the use of color, new types of urban, suburban and seaside group construction. It is not only in England that the possibility of such development and the force of such an analogy exist, but the English situation might encourage, as in some cases it has already done, specialization along one particular line quite different from what might evolve, for example, in America. Just such a specialization occurred in England in the seventeenth century, which was characterized by a dignified mastery of the large and the medium-sized house, after the international academic style had been successfully introduced and absorbed.

Conclusion

One can end a consideration of English architecture in the winter of 1937 not merely with the conclusion that its present achievement is almost unique and could hardly have been foretold even five years ago. One can also prognosticate that this achievement very probably represents the opening stage in an architectural development of prime creative significance, such as was initiated in the seventeenth century by the Restoration architects, and again along a very different line by the nineteenth century engineers in their bridges. This promise of Mackintosh's Glasgow School of Art may well be more than fulfilled and the loss of the Crystal Palace forgotten when English modern architecture is assayed after another generation of activity.

HENRY-RUSSELL HITCHCOCK, JR.

Plates

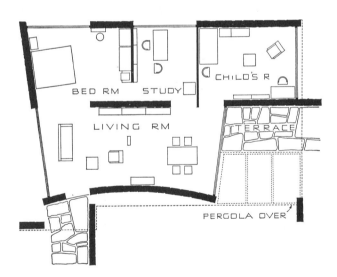

2 BREUER, Marcel: Pavilion at Royal Show, Bristol, for Messrs. P. E. Gane, Ltd., 1936. Exterior. (*In collaboration with* F. R. S. Yorke)

2 BREUER, Marcel: Pavilion at Royal Show, Bristol, for Messrs. P. E. Gane, Ltd., 1936. Living room. (*In collaboration with* F. R. S. Yorke)

3 BURNET, Sir John, TAIT & LORNE: Royal Masonic Hospital, Ravenscourt Park, London, 1934

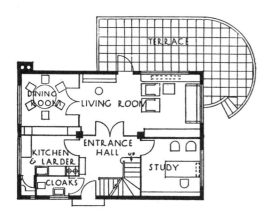

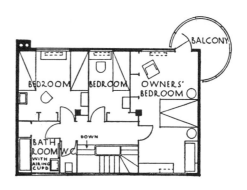

6 CHERMAYEFF, Serge: House at Rugby, 1934

Architect & Building News

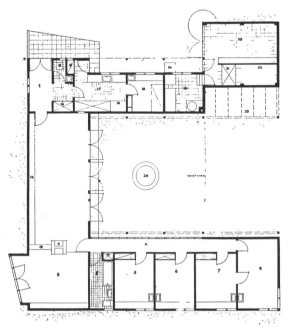

9 CHITTY, Anthony: House on Lloyd George's Estate, Churt, Surrey, 1935

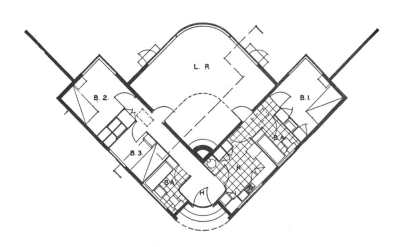

12 COATES, Wells: Sunspan Bungalow, Welwyn, 1935

11 COATES, Wells: Lawn Road Flats, Hampstead, London, 1934

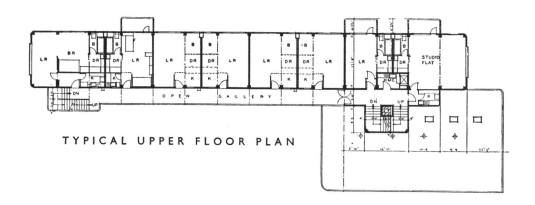

TYPICAL UPPER FLOOR PLAN

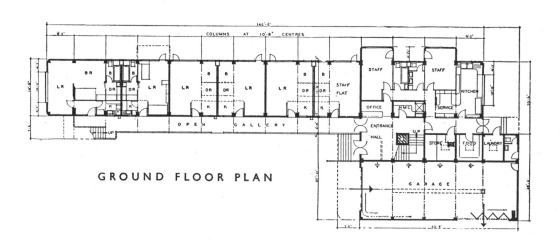

GROUND FLOOR PLAN

11 COATES, Wells: Lawn Road Flats, Hampstead, London, 1934

13 COATES, Wells: Embassy Court, Brighton, 1935

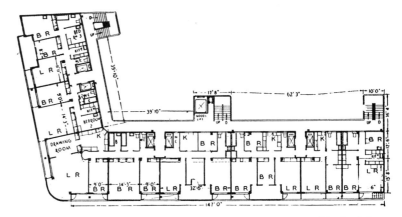

Typical floor

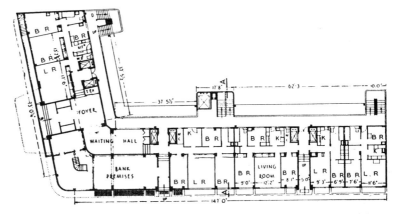

Ground floor

13 COATES, Wells: Embassy Court, Brighton, 1935

G. Baseden Butt

15 CONNELL, WARD & LUCAS: House at Platt, Kent, 1933

16 CONNELL, WARD & LUCAS: House at Bourne End, Buckinghamshire

18 EMBERTON, Joseph: Simpson's, Piccadilly, London, 1936

19 FRY, E. Maxwell: Sassoon House, Peckham, London, 1934. Rear façade.
(*In partnership with* Adams and Thompson)

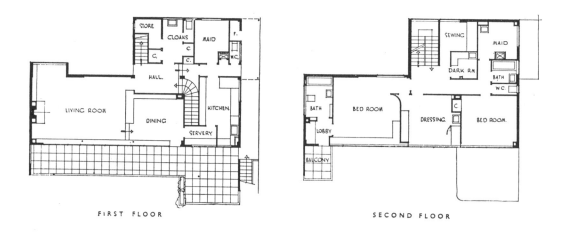

FIRST FLOOR

SECOND FLOOR

22 FRY, E. Maxwell: House in Frognal Way, Hampstead, London, 1936

22 FRY, E. Maxwell: House in Frognal Way, Hampstead, London, 1936. Living room

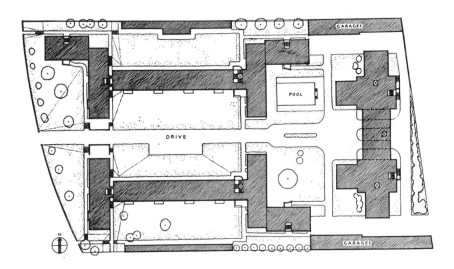

27 GIBBERD, Frederick: Pullman Court, Streatham, London, 1936. General view

27 GIBBERD, Frederick: Pullman Court, Streatham, London, 1936. One and two room flats

Architectural Review

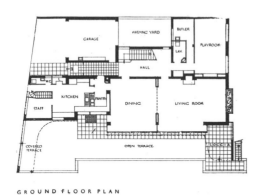

GROUND FLOOR PLAN

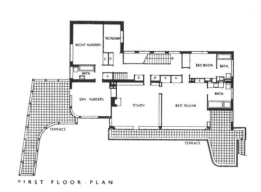

FIRST FLOOR PLAN

28 GROPIUS, Walter and FRY, E. Maxwell: House for Benn Levy, Church Street, Chelsea, London, 1936. Street façade. (House in distance by Mendelsohn & Chermayeff)

Architectural Review

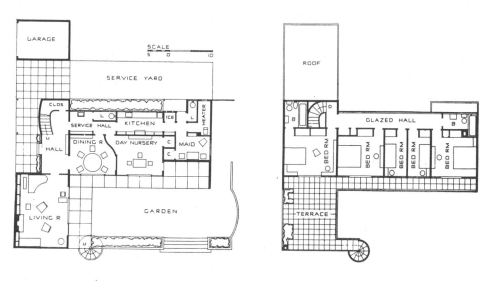

30 HARDING, Valentine: "Egypt End," Farnham Common, 1935. Garden façade
(*In association with* Tecton)

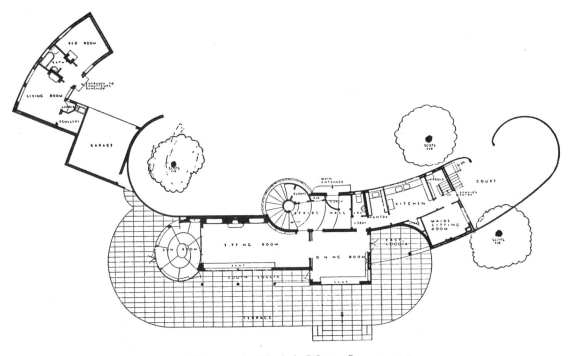

31 HILL, Oliver: House at Wentworth, Virginia Water, Surrey, 1935

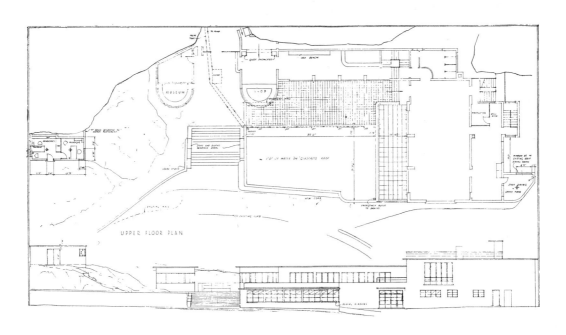

33 JELLICOE, Geoffrey Allan: The Caveman Restaurant, Cheddar Gorge, 1935

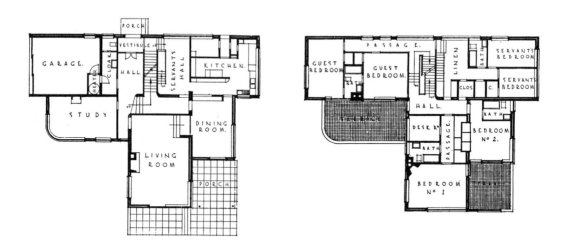

37 **LESCAZE**, William: Headmaster's House, Dartington Hall, Totnes, South Devon, 1931

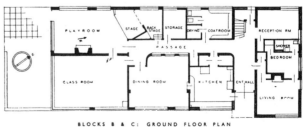

BLOCKS B & C: GROUND FLOOR PLAN

38 LESCAZE, William: Dormitories, Dartington Hall, Totnes, South Devon, 1934

40 LESCAZE, William: Estate Offices, Dartington Hall, Totnes, South Devon, 1935

Architectural Review

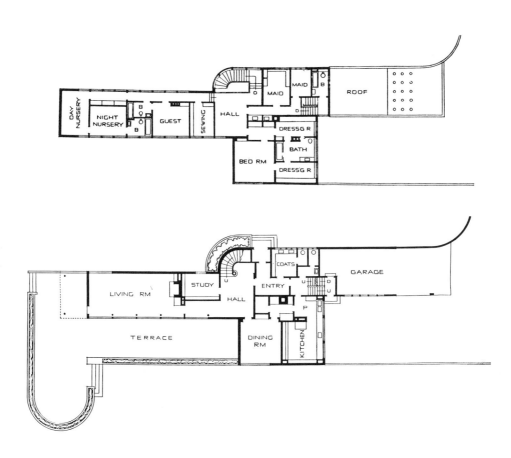

41 MENDELSOHN & CHERMAYEFF: House at Chalfont St. Giles, 1935

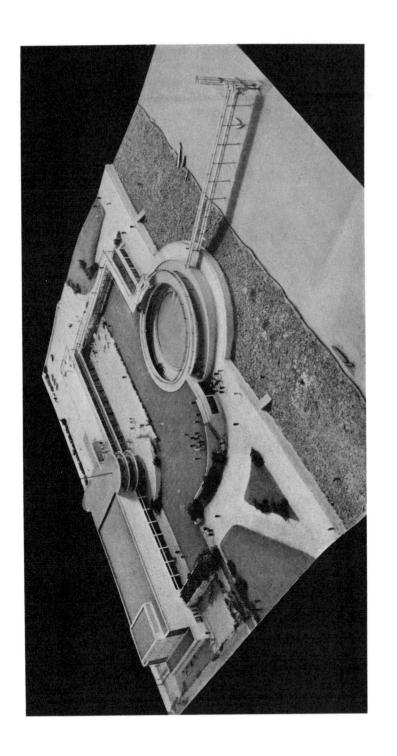

42 MENDELSOHN & CHERMAYEFF: De La Warr Pavilion, Bexhill-on-sea, 1935. Model

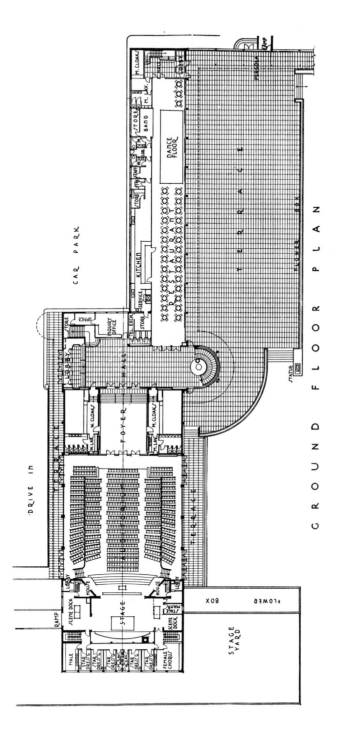

GROUND FLOOR PLAN

42 MENDELSOHN & CHERMAYEFF: *De La Warr Pavilion, Bexhill-on-sea, 1935*

42 MENDELSOHN & CHERMAYEFF: De La Warr Pavilion, Bexhill-on-sea, 1935. Ocean front façade

42 MENDELSOHN & CHERMAYEFF: De La Warr Pavilion, Bexhill-on-sea, 1935.
Street façade

42 MENDELSOHN & CHERMAYEFF: De La Warr Pavilion, Bexhill-on-sea, 1935.
Entrance hall toward stairway.

Architectural Review

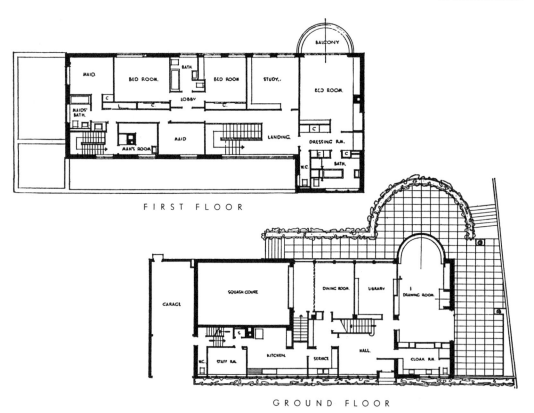

FIRST FLOOR

GROUND FLOOR

43 MENDELSOHN & CHERMAYEFF: House in Church Street, Chelsea, London, 1935. Street façade. (In the distance may be seen the house for Benn Levy by Gropius and Fry)

Architectural Review

44 NICHOLSON, Christopher: Augustus John's Studio, Fordingbridge, Hampshire, 1934

Architectural Review

47 PILICHOWSKI, A. V.: Whittinghame College, Brighton, 1936

GROUND FLOOR

FIRST FLOOR

49 SAMUEL, Godfrey (Samuel and Harding) : House in Bromley, Kent, 1935

51 SLATER AND MOBERLY; CRABTREE, W.: Peter Jones, Sloane Square, London, 1936
(Professor C. H. Reilly, consulting architect)

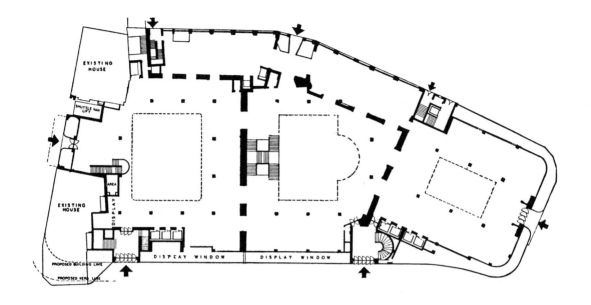

51 SLATER AND MOBERLY; CRABTREE, W.: Peter Jones, Sloane Square, London, 1936
  (Professor C. H. Reilly, consulting architect)

Architectural Review

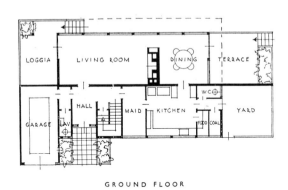

GROUND FLOOR

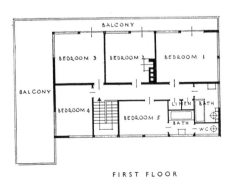

FIRST FLOOR

50 SISSON, Marshall: Gull Rock House, Cornwall, 1934

52 TECTON: Gorilla House, Regent's Park Zoo, London, 1931

John Havinden

53 TECTON: Penguin Pool, Regent's Park Zoo, London, 1933

54 TECTON: Flats at Highpoint, Highgate, London, 1933

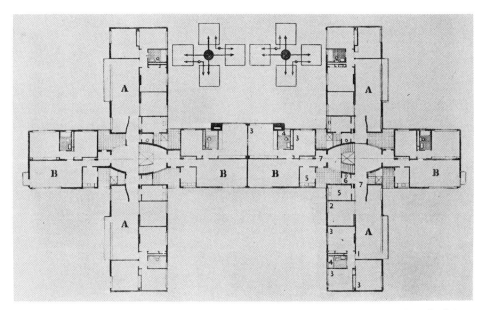

Typical floor

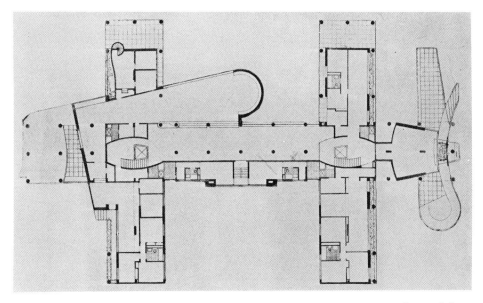

Ground floor

54 TECTON: Flats at Highpoint, Highgate, London, 1933

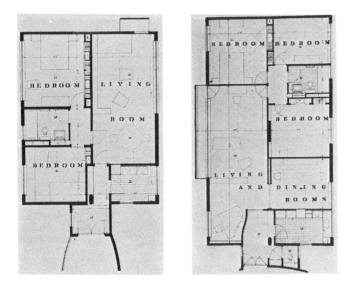

54 TECTON: Flats at Highpoint, Highgate, London, 1933. Foyer and plans of typical flats

Architects' Journal

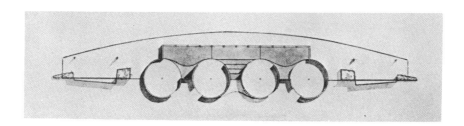

57 TECTON: Elephant House, Zoo at Whipsnade, 1934

Architect & Building News

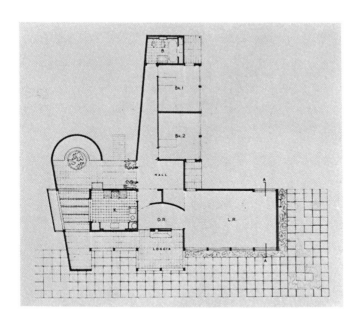

60 **TECTON**: House for B. Lubetkin, Whipsnade, 1935

Architect & Building News

61 TECTON: Weekend House, Whipsnade, 1935

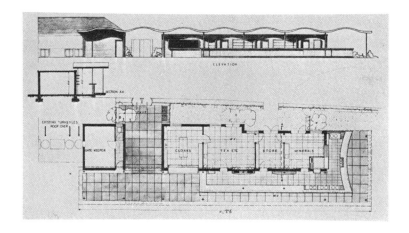

62 TECTON: North Gate, Regent's Park Zoo, London, 1936

63 WILLIAMS, Sir E. Owen: Warehouse for Messrs. Boots' Pure Drug Company, Ltd., Beeston, 1931-32

65 WILLIAMS, Sir E. Owen: Pioneer Health Centre, Peckham, London, 1935

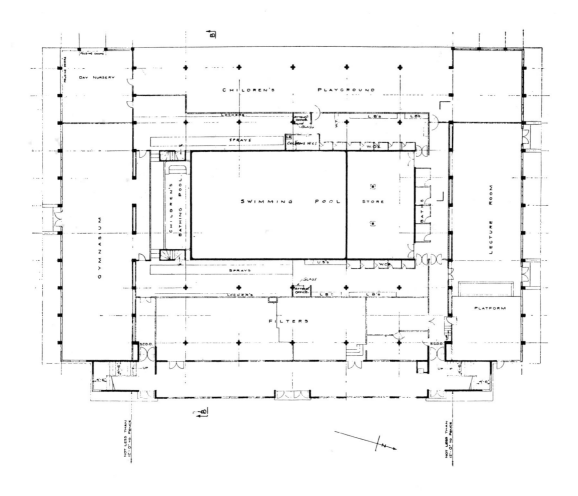

65 WILLIAMS, Sir E. Owen: Pioneer Health Centre, Peckham, London, 1935

Architectural Review

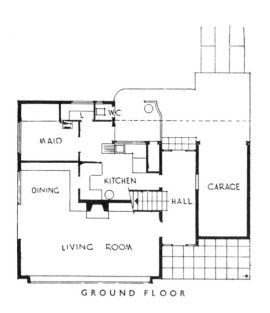

GROUND FLOOR

FIRST FLOOR

68 YORKE, F. R. S.: House at Iver, 1936

75 HEAPS, S. A.: Chiswick Park Station, District Line. (Adams, Holden & Pearson, consulting architects), 1934 or after

71 ADAMS, HOLDEN & PEARSON: Wood Green Station, Piccadilly Line, 1934 or after

72 ADAMS, HOLDEN & PEARSON: Southgate Station, Piccadilly Line, 1934 or after

Catalog of the Exhibition

ADAMS, HOLDEN and PEARSON,
F.F.R.I.B.A.

See UNDERGROUND STATIONS

BREUER, Marcel

Born in Pecs, Hungary, 1902. Studied architecture at the Staatliches Bauhaus in Weimar under Walter Gropius. Moved with the Bauhaus to Dessau and taught there from 1925 to 1928, the years of the Bauhaus' greatest activity. Although he has built several outstanding houses, he is perhaps best known for his invention of the now omnipresent tubular steel furniture (first chair at the Bauhaus, 1925, *cf. Machine Art,* The Museum of Modern Art, 1934, pl. 279, *Cubism and Abstract Art,* The Museum of Modern Art, 1936, pl. 165) and his exposition architecture (Werkbund Exposition, Paris, 1930, Bauaustellung, Berlin, 1931). Along with other Bauhaus masters (Gropius and Moholy-Nagy) he is now settled in London where he has formed an architectural partnership with F.R.S. Yorke.

In collaboration with F.R.S. Yorke

1 House at Clifton, Bristol, 1936
*2 Pavilion at Royal Show, Bristol, for Messrs. P. E. Gane, Ltd., 1936.

SIR JOHN BURNET, TAIT & LORNE

*3 Royal Masonic Hospital, Ravenscourt Park, London, 1934
4 Curzon Street Cinema, London, 1934
*5 Flats in Lowndes Street, London, *c.* 1936

CHERMAYEFF, Serge, F.R.I.B.A.

Born 1900, in the Caucasus. Educated in England, receiving at the age of twelve the gold, silver and bronze medals at the Royal Drawing Society. Then Harrow, after which he studied architecture in Europe from 1918-22. In 1922 went to the Argentine and returned to London in 1924 where he was designer in a decorator's firm until 1929 when he went with Waring and Gillow. Began independent practice of architecture in 1931. In 1933 formed partnership with Erich Mendelsohn. This partnership has recently been dissolved, each member continuing private practice.

*6 House at Rugby, 1934
7 Flat in Upper Brook Street, London, 1935
8 Broadcasting House, Birmingham

For work in collaboration with Erich Mendelsohn, *see* MENDELSOHN

CHITTY, Anthony, A.R.I.B.A.

Born Eton, England, 1907. After receiving a master's degree from Trinity College, Cambridge, he studied at the Architectural Association School. Was a member of Tecton from 1930 to 1935 when he left to enter private practice.

*9 House on Lloyd George's estate, Churt, Surrey, 1935
10 House at Bognor, Sussex, 1935

COATES, Wells

Born Tokyo, Japan, 1895. Educated privately in Japan. In 1913 he entered McGill University, Canada.

Four years of war service interrupted his scholastic career, but he returned to take a B.A. degree in 1920. Received a B.Sc. degree at the University of British Columbia in 1922 and in 1924 a Ph.D. in engineering at the University of London. From 1924 to 1930 he travelled and worked in offices in England, France, the United States and Canada, and in 1930 commenced private practice in London. Active in encouraging modern design, he was a founder member of the English section of the International Congress of Modern Architecture, known as the M.A.R.S. group. Besides the work illustrated, he has designed interiors, shops and was one of the group of architects who designed rooms for the B.B.C. He has also designed industrial products, ranging from hardware to pianos.

*11 Lawn Road Flats, Lawn Road, Hampstead, London, 1934
*12 Sunspan Bungalow, Lanercost Estate, Welwyn, Hertfordshire, 1935
*13 Embassy Court, Brighton, 1935
 14 Flat of the Architect, 1936

CONNELL, WARD AND LUCAS

CONNELL, Amyas, R.S.

Born Eltham, New Zealand, 1901. Educated in New Zealand and in England at London University. In 1926 received the Rome Scholarship in Architecture. Formed partnership with Basil R. Ward. Colin A. Lucas was taken into the firm at a later date.

WARD, Basil R., A.R.I.B.A.

Born New Zealand, 1902. Received his preliminary education in New Zealand, later attended London University. Awarded a Jarvis Studentship in Rome by the Royal Institute of British Architects in 1926.

LUCAS, Colin A.

Born London, 1906. Graduate of Cheltenham and Trinity College, Cambridge.

*15 House at Platt, St. Mary's Wrotham, Kent, 1933
*16 House at Bourne End, Buckinghamshire

CRABTREE, W., A.R.I.B.A.
See SLATER AND MOBERLY

DRAKE, Lindsey, W.A.T.
See TECTON

EMBERTON, Joseph, F.R.I.B.A.
 17 Timothy White's, Southsea, Hampshire
*18 Simpson's, Piccadilly, London, 1936

FRY, E. Maxwell, A.R.I.B.A.

Born Cheshire, England, 1899. Educated Liverpool Institute and University from which he received in 1924 his degree of B. Arch. with first class honors. In that year became Design Associate of the Royal Institute of British Architects. From 1927 to 1935 a partner in the firm of Adams, Thompson and Fry. In 1936 formed a partnership with Professor Walter Gropius. Founder member of Modern Architectural Research Group (M.A.R.S.) and a member of the Council of the Royal Institute of British Architects and the Housing Centre.

*19 Sassoon House, Peckham, London, 1934 (*in partnership with* Adams and Thompson)

96

20 House at Chipperfield, Hertfordshire, 1935, proposed

21 House at Chipperfield, Hertfordshire, 1935, executed

*22 "The Sun House," Frognal Way,
Hampstead, London, 1936

In partnership with Walter Gropius

23 Nursery School, Kensal Green Development, 1936

24 Flats for the Capitol Housing Association, Ltd., Ladbroke Grove Estate,
North Kensington, London, 1936-37

25 House at Combe, Kingston, Surrey,
1936-37

26 Sports Pavilion, Acton, 1936-37

GIBBERD, Frederick, A.I.A.A.

Born Coventry, England, 1908. Although he studied at a school of architecture, his formal education, archi-
tecturally speaking, was incomplete,
and he considers himself "mainly self-
taught." After travelling on the Continent, studying modern architecture
in Prague, Vienna, Budapest, The
Hague, Paris, etc., he commenced private practice in 1935 as a specialist in
low-rental flats on which subject he
has written many articles and reports.
In addition to Pullman Court, illustrated here, Mr. Gibberd has in construction two other flat developments.

*27 Pullman Court, Streatham, London,
1936

GROPIUS, Walter

Born Berlin, 1883. Studied architecture in Munich and Berlin. In 1918
was appointed director of the two
schools in Weimar that a year later
were to merge under the name "Bauhaus." In 1925 the Bauhaus moved to
Dessau at the invitation of that city
and Gropius began work on the

group of buildings that formed the
largest modern project at that time
in the world. No other school has ex-
erted through its theories as well as
its products so wide an influence on
architecture, art and industrial design. In 1928 Gropius resigned from
his post to enter private practice. In
1934 he came to London and, in 1936
entered into a partnership with Maxwell Fry. He has now accepted an ap-
pointment as Nelson Robinson, Jr.
Professor of Architecture at Harvard
University. (For further biography
see *Modern Architecture,* The Museum of Modern Art, 1932, pp. 57-70.)

In partnership with Maxwell Fry

*28 House for Benn Levy, Church Street,
Chelsea, London, 1936

29 Denham Laboratories, Ltd., Denham
near London, 1936.

HARDING, Valentine, A.R.I.B.A.

Born London, 1905. Graduate of Cor-
pus Christi College, Oxford, and the
Architectural Association School. In
the last year of his architectural studies he began private practice and in
1930 became one of the original partners of Tecton. In 1935 he resigned
and entered into partnership with
Godfrey Samuel, also formerly of
Tecton.

In association with TECTON

*30 "Egypt End," Egypt, Farnham Com-
mon, Bucks, 1935
See also GODFREY SAMUEL

HEAPS, S. A., F.R.I.B.A.
See UNDERGROUND STATIONS

HILL, Oliver, F.R.I.B.A.
Born London, 1887. Decided at age
of ten to become an architect. Edu-

cated at Uppingham School and afterwards spent eighteen months in builder's yard. In 1909 entered office of late William Flockhart as articled pupil, also attending evening classes at Architectural Association and studying traditional styles. In 1912 commenced private practice, which was interrupted by four years' war service. Earlier practice devoted to domestic work, garden design, furniture, etc., based on traditional styles, later work more concerned with contemporary design and modern methods of fabrication.

*31 House at Wentworth, Virginia Water, Surrey, 1935
32 "The Leas," Frinton-on-sea, Essex, 1935

JELLICOE, Geoffrey Allan, F.R.I.B.A., A.I.L.A.

Born London, 1900. Studied at Cheltenham College and Architectural Association. Bernard Webb student at the British School at Rome. Author of several books on gardens.

*33 The Caveman Restaurant, Cheddar Gorge, 1935

KAUFMANN, Eugen C.

Born Frankfort-on-Main, 1892. Studied at the Technical High Schools of Munich and Berlin and graduated from the latter as Dipl. Ing. in 1914. Began architectural practice in 1919. Director of Housing in Frankfort from 1925-31; Technical Consultant for Housing, Town and Regional planning to Russian State Trusts from 1931-33. In 1933 came to London where he resumed private practice. Since 1936 he has served as Director

of Research to the Housing Centre.

34 House at Victoria Road, Wimbledon, 1935
35 King Alfred School, North End Road, Hampstead, 1936
36 Houses at Angmering-on-sea, 1936

LESCAZE, William

Born Geneva, Switzerland, 1896. Studied at the Ecole Polytechnique Fédérale in Zurich, 1915-1919, receiving the degree of Master of Architecture. He came to the United States in 1920 and went first to Cleveland, Ohio, where he remained until 1923. In that year he opened his own office in New York. In 1929 formed a partnership with George Howe, during which period the firm built the Philadelphia Saving Fund Society, the first skyscraper of true modern design in America. This partnership was terminated in 1933, each continuing private practice.

*37 Headmaster's House, Dartington Hall, Totnes, South Devon, 1931
*38 Dormitories, Dartington Hall, Totnes, South Devon, 1934
39 House for Kurt Jooss, Dartington Hall, Totnes, South Devon, 1935
*40 Estate offices, Dartington Hall, Totnes, South Devon, 1935

LUBETKIN, Berthold
See TECTON

LUCAS, Colin A.
See CONNELL, WARD AND LUCAS

MENDELSOHN, Erich

Born 1887 in East Prussia. Studied at the Technische Hochschule, Charlottenburg and also in Munich. Practiced from 1911-1914 in Munich and

98

from 1914-1933 in Berling. Among his outstanding works of this period are the Einstein Tower, Potsdam (1919), Schocken Department Stores (1925-30) and the Columbus House (1931). Came to London in 1933 where he worked in partnership with Serge Chermayeff until 1937. He has also been very active in Palestine. Author of *Architecture in Steel and Reinforced Concrete,* and *New Architecture, 1919, America, Architect's Picture Book, 1923, Russia, Europe, America, 1926,* and *The Creative Spirit of the World Crisis,* 1932.

In collaboration with Serge Chermayeff

*41 House at Chalfont St. Giles, Bucks, 1935
*42 De La Warr Pavilion, Bexhill-on-sea, Sussex, 1935
*43 House in Church Street, Chelsea, London, 1936
  See also SERGE CHERMAYEFF

MOBERLY, A. H., F.R.I.B.A.
See SLATER AND MOBERLY

NICHOLSON, Christopher
Born London, 1904. Studied at Cambridge University School of Architecture from 1923. Anderson and Webb University Scholar in Architecture, 1925. Davison scholarship from Cambridge University to Princeton University, 1926-27. Worked in the office of Val Myer and Watson Hart in London, 1931-32.

*44 Augustus John's Studio, Fordingbridge, Hampshire, 1934
 45 London Gliding Club, Dunstable Downs, Bedfordshire, 1936

PILICHOWSKI, A. V., A.R.I.B.A.

 46 Highfield Court, Golders Green, 1935
*47 Whittinghame College, Brighton, 1936
 48 Flats, Earl's Terrace, Edwards Square, Kensington

SAMUEL, Godfrey, A.R.I.B.A.

Born London, 1904. After receiving his degree from Balliol College, Oxford, he studied at the Architectural Association School. Was one of the original Tecton partners from the foundation of the firm in 1930 to 1935 when he resigned to form a partnership with Valentine Harding.

In collaboration with Valentine Harding
*49 "By the Links," Lodge Road, Bromley, Kent, 1935
  See also VALENTINE HARDING

SISSON, Marshall, F.R.I.B.A.

Born Gloucester, England, 1897. Received his professional education at University of London School of Architecture. Awarded Jarvis Studentship by the Royal Institute of British Architects in 1924. Studied at the British School in Rome from 1924 until 1927 when he received the Duveen Fellowship for travel and study of architecture in America. Here he studied in the office of John Russell Pope for six months. In 1928 he returned to London to start private practice.

*50 Gull Rock House, Carlyon Bay, St. Austell, Cornwall, 1934

SKINNER, R. T. F.
See TECTON

SLATER and MOBERLY

SLATER, J. Alan, F.R.I.B.A.
M.A., Cambridge

MOBERLY, A. H., F.R.I.B.A.
M.A., Cambridge

CRABTREE, W., A.R.I.B.A.
*51 Peter Jones, Sloane Square, London,
1936

Consulting architect: Professor C. H.
Reilly, F.R.I.B.A.; formerly Professor
of Architecture, Liverpool University.

TECTON, A.A.R.I.B.A.

LUBETKIN, Berthold
Born in Caucasus, 1901. Studied first
in Moscow and then in Paris at the
Ecole Speciale d'Architecture, Atelier
Perret, Ecole des Beaux Arts, Sor-
bonne Town Planning Institute, Institute Politechnique. Won first prize
in the competition for the Ural Poly-
technical University, U.S.S.R., 1925,
and also a prize in the competition
for the Palace of the Soviets in Moscow, 1931. Practiced architecture in
France before coming to England in
1930, where he formed the firm
known as Tecton. Among the mem-
bers have been Michael Dugdale,
Godfrey Samuel, Valentine Harding,
and Anthony Chitty.

DRAKE, Lindsey W. A. T.
Born London, 1909. Studied at
the Architectural Association School
where he held in 1928 the Holloway
Scholarship.

SKINNER, R. T. F.
Born Malayo, 1908. Studied at the
Architectural Association School.
One of the founders of the Archi-
tects and Technicians Organization.

*52 Gorilla House, Regent's Park Zoo,
London, 1931
*53 Penguin Pool, Regent's Park Zoo,
London, 1933
*54 Flats at Highpoint, Highgate, Lon-
don, 1933
55 Giraffe House, Zoo at Whipsnade,
1934
56 Restaurant, Zoo at Whipsnade, 1934
*57 Elephant House, Zoo at Whipsnade,
1934
58 Elephant House Waiting Room, Zoo
at Whipsnade, 1934
59 Waiting Room at entrance, Zoo at
Whipsnade, 1935
*60 House for B. Lubetkin, Whipsnade,
1935
*61 Weekend house, Whipsnade, 1935
*62 North Gate, Regent's Park Zoo, Lon-
don, 1936

WARD, Basil R., A.R.I.B.A.
see CONNELL, WARD AND LUCAS

WELCH and LAUDER, F.F.R.I.B.A.
See UNDERGROUND STATIONS

WILLIAMS, Sir E. Owen, K.B.E.
Born London, 1890. In 1906 began
studying to be an engineer and received his B.Sc. with first class honors. Has specialized in reinforced concrete and in 1919 commenced private
practice as Consulting Engineer. Has
designed bridges as well as buildings
of all types. Until 1929 usually col-
laborated with architects but in that
year decided to undertake the entire

work on Dorchester House, London and since that time has acted in the dual capacity of architect and engineer.

*63 Warehouse for Messrs. Boots' Pure Drug Company, Ltd., Beeston, 1931-32

64 Portland Cement Co., Ltd., Laboratory, West Thurrock, 1933

*65 Pioneer Health Centre, Peckham, London, 1935

66 Warehouse and Office Building for Messrs. Lilley and Skinner, Ltd., Pentonville Rd., London, 1936

YORKE, F. R. S., A.R.I.B.A.
Born Stratford-on-Avon, England, 1906. Graduate of the School of Architecture, Birmingham; also studied town planning at the Birmingham University. Author of *The Modern House,* 1934, perhaps the best English book on modern architecture, and editor of *Specifications.* Among his completed work are several private houses, a factory at Redditch and masters' houses at Eton.

67 House at Nast Hyde, Hatfield, Hertfordshire, 1935

*68 House in High Street, Iver, 1936
For work in collaboration with Marcel Breuer, see BREUER

UNDERGROUND STATIONS

For the London Passenger Transport Board

69 Arno's Grove Station, Piccadilly Line, 1934 or before
Architects: Adams, Holden and Pearson, F.F.R.I.B.A.

70 Boston Manor Station, Piccadilly and District Lines, 1934 or after
Architects: Adams, Holden and Pearson, F.F.R.I.B.A.

*71 Wood Green Station, Piccadilly Line, 1934 or after
Architects: Adams, Holden and Pearson, F.F.R.I.B.A.

*72 Southgate Station, Piccadilly Line, 1934 or after
Architects: Adams, Holden and Pearson, F.F.R.I.B.A.

73 Osterley Station, Piccadilly and District Lines, 1934 or after
Architect: S. A. Heaps, F.R.I.B.A. Adams, Holden and Pearson, F.F.R.I.B.A., consulting architects

74 South Harrow Station, Metropolitan and Piccadilly Lines, 1934 or after
Architect: S. A. Heaps, F.R.I.B.A. Adams, Holden and Pearson, F.F.R.I.B.A., consulting architects

*75 Chiswick Park Station, District Line, 1934 or after
Architect: S. A. Heaps, F.R.I.B.A. Adams, Holden and Pearson, F.F.R.I.B.A., consulting architects

76 Enfield West Station, Piccadilly Line, 1934 or after
Architect: C. H. James, F.R.I.B.A. Adams, Holden and Pearson, F.F.R.I.B.A., consulting architects

77 Park Royal Station, 1934 or after
Architects: Welch and Lauder, F.F.R.I.B.A.

It is unfortunate that the material compiled by the Housing Centre arrived too late to be catalogued. This includes a brief history of Housing and the development of Town Planning in England. The data for this section was assembled by the Housing Centre under the direction of Philip R. Rathbone, Secretary.

THREE THOUSAND COPIES OF THIS CATALOG WERE

PRINTED FOR THE TRUSTEES OF THE MUSEUM OF

MODERN ART BY THE SPIRAL PRESS · NEW YORK

091195